CONTENTS

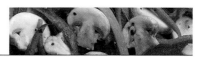

Outdoor Pleasures   4

Barbecue Cooking   36

Salad Main Attractions   56

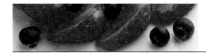

Fresh Fruit Finales   68

Index   80

OUTDOOR
PLEASURES

As the days grow longer and warmer, we find ourselves tempted to move our meals outdoors — whether to the backyard patio or apartment balcony, or to a nearby park.

But there is no reason such meals should not be just as exciting and palate-pleasing as the meals we eat indoors. For example, a patio meal starring cold poached salmon (as shown on page 25) is an elegant way to entertain friends for a long and lazy summer lunch.

And a simple summer picnic will turn into a memorable event if you include a sophisticated rabbit terrine or a homemade pâté along with the traditional cold chicken and potato salad.

If you do most of your meal or picnic preparation in the cool of the evening or early morning, plan some simple side dishes and salads, and pick up dessert from a good bakery, summer entertaining will also be easy on the cook!

EASY SUMMER
COOKING

TORMONT

Graphic Design: Zapp

This edition published in 1996 by:
Tormont Publications Inc.
338 Saint Antoine St. East
Montreal, Canada H2Y 1A3
Tel. (514) 954-1441
Fax (514) 954-5086

ISBN 2-7641-0101-5
Printed in Canada

Peperonata (top, page 32), Rabbit Pistachio Terrine, Devilled Lamb Chops (page 6)

Devilled Lamb Chops

8	lamb chops	8
1 tsp	salt	5 mL
1 tsp	dry mustard	5 mL
1 tsp	ground ginger	5 mL
1 tsp	curry powder	5 mL
2 tsp	sugar	10 mL
2 tbsp	tomato relish	30 mL
2 tbsp	fruit chutney	30 mL
1 tbsp	Worcestershire sauce	15 mL

◆ ◆ ◆

1 Trim excess fat from chops and rub well with mixed spices and sugar. Let stand at room temperature to marinate for 1 hour.

2 Cook chops under a preheated broiler for 3 minutes on each side. Place relish, chutney and Worcestershire sauce in a bowl, mix well and spread over chops. Cook for 2 minutes more or until cooked as desired.

Serves 4

Note: These lamb chops make interesting finger food for picnics. Let cooked chops cool slightly before wrapping them, and pack plenty of napkins.

Rabbit Pistachio Terrine

1 1/2 lbs	boneless rabbit meat, ground	675 g
1 lb	ground sausage	450 g
1 lb	ground pork	450 g
1 1/2 cups	dried breadcrumbs	375 mL
1	small onion, finely chopped	1
1	garlic clove, crushed	1
1/2 tsp	dried thyme	2 mL
2 tbsp	Pernod	30 mL
1 tbsp	salt	15 mL
1/4 tsp	freshly ground black pepper	1 mL
1	egg, beaten	1
1/4 lb	chopped pistachio nuts or walnuts	110 g
1/2 lb	bacon slices	225 g

◆ ◆ ◆

1 Preheat oven to 350°F (180°C). Place ground rabbit in a large bowl with sausage, pork and breadcrumbs. Add onion, garlic, thyme, Pernod, salt, pepper, egg, and nuts. Mix well with a wooden spoon.

2 Line a 10 cup (2.5 L) terrine or loaf pan with bacon. Spoon rabbit mixture into pan and level surface. Cut remaining bacon into thin strips and arrange on top of mixture in a crisscross pattern. Cover tightly with foil or lid and bake for 1 1/2 hours.

3 Remove from oven, remove lid and place a weight on top of terrine. Let stand until cool, then refrigerate overnight. Serve sliced with crusty bread and pickled gherkins.

Serves 10-12

Veal and Spinach Terrine

8	large spinach leaves	8
3 tbsp	butter	45 mL
2	garlic cloves, crushed	2
1	onion, finely chopped	1
4	slices bacon, chopped	4
1 1/3 lbs	finely ground veal	600 g
1 tbsp	grated orange zest	15 mL
2 tbsp	chopped green onions	30 mL
2 tsp	chopped fresh thyme	10 mL
1 1/2 tbsp	drained green peppercorns	25 mL
1 tbsp	dry red wine	15 mL
2 cups	day-old breadcrumbs	500 mL
2	eggs, beaten	2
14 oz	can apricot halves, drained	398 mL
1 tbsp	fresh lemon juice	15 mL
1 tbsp	apricot jam	15 mL

♦ ◆ ♦

1 Put spinach leaves in a large bowl, cover with boiling water and set aside for 1 minute. Drain, refresh under cold water and drain again.

2 Line bottom and sides of an 8 inch (20 cm) cake pan with spinach, reserving enough to cover top.

3 Melt butter in a large saucepan, add garlic and onion and fry for 2-3 minutes. Stir in bacon and cook for 2 minutes more. Stir in veal and orange zest; cook, stirring constantly, for 10 minutes. Cool mixture slightly, then stir in green onions, thyme, peppercorns, wine, breadcrumbs and eggs. Mix until well combined.

4 Press mixture firmly into prepared pan. Cover with reserved spinach leaves and bake for 40 minutes. Let cool in pan before slicing.

5 Make an apricot sauce by blending or processing apricots with lemon juice and jam until smooth. Press through a sieve. Serve with terrine.

Serves 8

Spicy Meatballs *with* Coriander Sauce

2/3 cup	raisins	165 mL
1 lb	lean ground lamb	450 g
2 tbsp	pine nuts	30 mL
1	small onion, finely chopped	1
1 tbsp	chopped fresh parsley	15 mL
1	garlic clove, crushed	1
1 tsp	ground cumin	5 mL
1 tsp	ground cinnamon	5 mL
	assorted fresh vegetables for dipping	

CORIANDER SAUCE

3/4 cup	plain yogurt	185 mL
1	garlic clove, crushed	1
3 tbsp	fresh coriander leaves	45 mL

1 Preheat oven to 400°F (200°C). Soak raisins in hot water for 15 minutes, drain and chop coarsely. Combine raisins, lamb, pine nuts, onion, parsley, garlic, cumin and cinnamon in a bowl and mix well. Shape mixture into 25 balls and place in a single layer on an ungreased baking sheet. Bake, uncovered, for 30 minutes or until cooked through.

2 Combine sauce ingredients and let stand for 30 minutes. Serve meatballs hot or cold with dipping sauce, vegetables and toasted bagel thins.

Serves 4-6

♦ ♦ ♦

Bruschetta

1	loaf Italian bread	1
1/2 cup	light olive oil	125 mL
2-3	garlic cloves, peeled and cut in half	2-3
2	large ripe, firm tomatoes, diced	2
2	green onions, thinly sliced	2
6	basil leaves, chopped	6
2 tbsp	balsamic vinegar	30 mL
1 tsp	freshly ground black pepper	5 mL

1 Cut loaf into 3/4 inch (2 cm) slices. Brush olive oil on both sides of slices then rub with garlic. Place under a preheated broiler and toast both sides until golden.

2 Mix tomatoes with green onions and basil, add vinegar and pepper and toss lightly. Heap spoonfuls of tomato mixture onto warm bread slices and serve immediately.

Serves 8

♦ ♦ ♦

Escabeche of Tongue

1	large (or 2 small) ox tongue	1
6	each whole allspice, whole cloves black peppercorns	6
1	onion, sliced	1
1	bouquet garni	1
1	carrot, quartered	1
1	celery stalk, cut into pieces	1

EGG SAUCE

4	garlic cloves, chopped	4
1/3 cup	olive oil	85 mL
3 tbsp	wine vinegar	45 mL
1/2 cup	finely chopped fresh parsley	125 mL
2	hard-boiled eggs, finely chopped	2
	dash Tabasco sauce	
	salt and freshly ground black pepper	

◆ ◆ ◆

1. Rinse tongue, curl it into a deep saucepan and cover with cold water. Add remaining ingredients except egg sauce, to pan and bring to a boil. Reduce heat to low, cover and simmer for 2-3 hours or until tongue is tender.

2. Allow tongue to cool for 1 hour in liquid. Remove root, skin, and any bones. Place on a flat plate, cover with plastic wrap and chill.

3. To make sauce, place garlic and olive oil in a bowl and beat in vinegar and Tabasco sauce until mixture is thick and creamy. Stir in parsley and eggs and season to taste with salt and pepper.

4. Slice tongue and arrange in a serving dish. Spoon sauce over and toss lightly to coat. Cover with plastic wrap and chill overnight before serving, garnished with more parsley.

Serves 8

TIP: *A bouquet garni is an array of fresh or dried herbs tied together. The classic combination is thyme, parsley and bay leaves.*

Salad Contadina

1 lb	new potatoes, cooked and sliced	450 g
1 lb	green beans, cooked	450 g
19 oz	can cannellini beans, rinsed and drained	540 mL
3	tomatoes, quartered	3
1	onion, sliced and separated into rings	1
2 tbsp	chopped fresh basil	30 mL

VINAIGRETTE

1/2 cup	olive oil	125 mL
2 tbsp	wine vinegar	30 mL
1 tsp	Dijon mustard	5 mL
1	garlic clove, crushed	1
	salt and freshly ground black pepper	

◆ ◆ ◆

1. To make dressing, place oil, vinegar, mustard, garlic and salt and pepper to taste in a screwtop jar and shake well to combine.

2. Place potatoes, and all beans in a salad bowl, add dressing and toss well to coat. Decorate salad with tomatoes and onions and sprinkle with basil.

Serves 6

Country-Style Pâté

2 lbs	ground pork and veal	1 kg
1 lb	fresh pork fat, ground or finely chopped	450 g
1 tbsp	salt	15 mL
1 tsp	freshly ground black pepper	5 mL
2 tsp	chopped fresh thyme	10 mL
2 tsp	chopped fresh oregano	10 mL
1 tsp	ground allspice	5 mL
1 tsp	dried tarragon	5 mL
4	garlic cloves, chopped	4
1/2 cup	cognac or brandy	125 mL
1/4 cup	dry vermouth or sherry	60 mL
4	eggs, lightly beaten	4
1	onion, finely chopped, sautéed in butter until soft and drained	1
1/2 lb	chicken livers, trimmed and quartered	225 g
3 oz	fresh walnut pieces	90 g
6	thin bacon slices	6
2	bay leaves	2
3	whole juniper berries	3

◆ ◆ ◆

1 Place ground pork and veal mixture in a large bowl with pork fat, salt, pepper, thyme, oregano, allspice, tarragon, garlic, cognac, vermouth, eggs and sautéed onion. Mix thoroughly without overworking mixture, then lightly fold in livers and walnuts.

2 Preheat oven to 350°F (180°C). Line base and sides of a 9 x 4 x 3 1/2 inch (23 x 10 x 9 cm) loaf pan with bacon, allowing ends to hang over sides. Pack meat mixture into pan, pressing out air pockets and slightly mounding center. Top with bay leaves and juniper berries.

3 Fold bacon ends over meat, then cover with aluminum foil, pressing snugly to seal. Place pan in a larger baking dish filled with enough boiling water to come halfway up sides of the pan. Bake for 2 1/2 hours.

4 Remove pan from water, top with a plate, then a heavy weight, and set aside to cool for several hours. Remove weight and plate and refrigerate until cold.

5 Remove pâté from loaf pan, scrape surfaces clean and clean the loaf pan. Return pâté to clean pan. Refrigerate at least 2 days before serving to allow flavors to mellow. Serve sliced at room temperature.

Serves 10

Parsley Tongue Mold

1 lb	whole ox tongue, corned or fresh	450 g
6	whole cloves	6
1	bouquet garni (see Tip page 10)	1
1	onion, sliced	1
1	carrot, sliced	1
1	celery stalk, sliced	1
1/2 tsp	salt	2 mL
1 lb	ham steak, cubed	450 g
1 cup	chicken stock	250 mL
1 cup	dry white wine	250 mL
1/2 cup	finely chopped fresh parsley	125 mL
2 tbsp	gelatine	30 mL
1-2 tbsp	wine vinegar	15-30 mL
	freshly ground black pepper and nutmeg	

◆ ◆ ◆

1 Place tongue in a saucepan and cover with water. Add cloves, bouquet garni, onion, carrot, celery and salt. Bring slowly to a boil, skim, then cover and simmer for 2-3 hours or until tongue is tender. Remove from heat and let cool.

2 Carefully remove skin, fat and any bones from tongue. Cut lengthwise into thick slices, then into small cubes.

3 Place tongue and ham cubes in saucepan, add stock and wine and season to taste with pepper and nutmeg. Bring to a boil, then reduce heat and simmer for 15 minutes. Drain cubes, reserving liquid. Arrange cubes in a 5-6 cup (1.25-1.5 L) loaf pan or bowl which has been rinsed out with water and lightly dusted with parsley.

4 Soften gelatine in a little water and dissolve into reserved hot liquid. Add remaining parsley and vinegar. Cool until mixture is syrupy, then pour over cubes in mold. Chill until set, at least 4 hours or overnight. Unmold and cut into thick slices. Serve with fine mustard.

Serves 8

Pissaladière

2 cups	all-purpose flour	500 mL
1/4 tsp	ground cinnamon	1 mL
6 tbsp	butter, cut into pieces	90 mL
4-5 tbsp	cold water	60-75 mL

PISSALADIÈRE FILLING

1/3 cup	olive oil	85 mL
2 lbs	onions, thinly sliced	1 kg
3	large garlic cloves, crushed	3
4 cups	canned tomatoes	1 L
1 tsp	sugar	5 mL
2-3	sprigs fresh thyme and oregano or	2-3
	1/2 tsp (2 mL) each dried thyme and oregano	
2 tbsp	tomato paste	30 mL
2	2 oz (55 g) cans flat anchovy fillets	2
10	black olives, halved	10
	uncooked rice	

♦ ♦ ♦

1 Place flour and cinnamon in a bowl. Cut in butter with a pastry cutter or knife until mixture resembles breadcrumbs. Add water and mix to a dough. Knead gently, wrap and chill for 30 minutes.

2 Heat oil in a skillet, add onion and garlic and cook, stirring, for 20 minutes or until onions are soft, but not brown. Place tomatoes, sugar and herbs in a saucepan and simmer until reduced to 1 cup (250 mL). Remove herb sprigs (if using). Stir in tomato paste and cooked onion.

3 Preheat oven to 375°F (190°C). Roll out pastry on a floured surface and with it line a greased baking pan. Cover pastry with wax paper, fill with rice and bake for 10 minutes. Remove rice and paper and cook for 5 minutes.

4 Raise oven temperature to 400°F (200°C). Spread tomato mixture over dough. Halve anchovies lengthwise and arrange on top in a crisscross pattern. Place an olive half in center of each diamond. Bake for 25 minutes or until cooked and golden. Serve warm.

Serves 8

Spicy Grilled Chicken

4 1/2 lbs	chicken drumsticks or pieces	2 kg
1	small onion, grated	1
2 tsp	salt	10 mL
1 tsp	freshly ground black pepper	5 mL
2 tsp	crushed garlic	10 mL
2 tsp	chili pepper paste or 1 fresh red chili pepper, finely chopped	10 mL
1 tbsp	brown sugar	15 mL
1 tbsp	lemon juice	15 mL
1 tbsp	vegetable oil	15 mL
2 tbsp	soy sauce	30 mL

♦ ♦ ♦

1 Score skin and flesh of the chicken and place in a shallow dish. Combine remaining ingredients in a bowl. Rub mixture into chicken, cover and let stand 2 hours at room temperature or overnight in refrigerator.

2 Cook chicken on a rack under a preheated broiler for 5-8 minutes on each side or until tender.

Serves 6

TIP: This chicken dish can also be cooked on the barbecue.

Chicken Tourtière

PASTRY

3 cups	all-purpose flour	750 mL
1/2 lb	unsalted butter	225 g
1	egg yolk mixed with 1 1/2 tbsp (25 mL) water	1

FILLING

3/4 cup	short-grain rice	185 mL
1 1/2 cups	water	375 mL
1 1/2 lbs	chicken thighs and drumsticks, boned and skinned	675 g
1 lb	boneless chicken breast fillets	450 g
1	bunch green onions, finely chopped	1
2 tsp	grated lemon rind	10 mL
2 tbsp	lemon juice	30 mL
1	egg, beaten	1
	salt and freshly ground black pepper	
4	hard-boiled eggs	4
	beaten egg for glazing	

♦ ♦ ♦

1 Sift flour into a large bowl. Cut butter into small pieces and then into flour with a pastry cutter or knife until mixture resembles coarse breadcrumbs.

2 Make a well in center of the flour mixture, add combined egg yolk and water and lightly mix to make a firm dough. Knead dough on a lightly floured surface until smooth. Wrap in plastic wrap and chill for 20-30 minutes.

3 To make filling, cook rice in water in covered saucepan over low heat until rice is tender and all liquid is absorbed.

4 Reserve about 1/2 the chicken breast meat and cut the rest, along with the thigh and drumstick meat, into cubes. Place cubes, in batches, in a food processor and process until ground.

5 Preheat oven to 350°F (180°C). Place ground chicken in a large bowl, add rice, green onions, lemon rind, lemon juice, egg, salt and pepper to taste and mix well to combine.

6 Roll out three-quarters of the pastry to line a deep loaf pan (or use a quiche pan or springform with a removable base), allowing pastry to slightly overhang rim. Cover pastry with half of rice mixture. Cut reserved chicken into long thick strips and place half the strips lengthwise on top of rice. Arrange hard-boiled eggs down center. Top with remaining chicken strips, then remaining rice mixture.

7 Roll out remaining pastry to cover filling, trim edges and pinch together to seal. Make a small cut in center and decorate, if desired, with pastry scraps. Brush with egg glaze and bake for 1-1 1/2 hours or until filling is cooked and pastry is well-browned. Cool to room temperature, then refrigerate until cold before removing from mold and slicing.

Serves 10

Oven-Fried Chicken

6	chicken drumsticks	6
2/3 cup	plain low-fat yogurt	165 mL
1 tsp	lemon juice	5 mL
2 tbsp	apricot or peach chutney	30 mL
1 1/4 cups	dried breadcrumbs	310 mL
	parsley sprigs for garnish	

◆ ◆ ◆

1 Preheat oven to 350°F (180°C). Purée yogurt, lemon juice and chutney in a blender or food processor and transfer mixture to a shallow bowl. Spread out breadcrumbs in a second bowl.

2 Coat each drumstick in yogurt mixture, then roll in breadcrumbs. Arrange on a baking sheet and bake for 45 minutes or until cooked through. Garnish and serve.

Makes 6

TIP: This is an easy recipe to double or triple. Just be sure to use a large enough baking pan to hold the chicken in a single layer.

Roast Chicken Fantasia

2	3 lb (1.5 kg) chickens	2
2	bacon slices, halved	2
6	fresh sage leaves	6
4	fresh rosemary sprigs	4
2 tbsp	each butter and oil	30 mL
12	thin slices prosciutto or ham	12
	salt	
2	large brown paper bags	2

◆ ◆ ◆

1 Remove excess fat from chickens. Season cavities with salt to taste, then fill each with half the bacon, sage and rosemary. Truss chickens with string.

2 Heat half the butter and oil in a skillet over moderately high heat and quickly brown 1 chicken on all sides. Repeat with other chicken. Remove from pan, cool slightly and then drape each chicken with prosciutto or ham.

3 Preheat oven to 350°F (180°C). Place each bird in a bag, brush bags with oil and tie securely closed with string. Place bags in an oiled baking dish and bake for 15 minutes. Pierce bags once or twice with a sharp knife and continue cooking for 1 hour.

4 Remove from oven and cut away bags, allowing juices to drain onto a heated serving plate. Line plate with prosciutto or ham pieces, and arrange chicken on top, whole or cut up. Serve with new potatoes.

Serves 6-8

Chicken Tonnato

2 1/2 cups	chicken stock	625 mL
1	celery stalk, sliced	1
1	onion, quartered	1
2	fresh parsley sprigs	2
1	bay leaf	1
6	black peppercorns	6
6	boneless chicken breast fillets	6
	lemon wedges, whole capers, black olives and parsley	

Tuna Sauce

6 oz	can tuna in oil	180 g
5	anchovy fillets	5
3 tbsp	lemon juice	45 mL
3 tbsp	capers	45 mL
1 1/2 cups	olive oil	375 mL
1 1/3 cups	mayonnaise	330 mL
	freshly ground black pepper	

♦ ◆ ♦

1 Place stock, celery, onion, parsley sprigs, bay leaf and peppercorns in a large saucepan. Bring to a boil and boil for 3-5 minutes. Add chicken, reduce heat, cover and gently poach for 6-8 minutes or until chicken is just tender. Remove from heat and set aside to cool in liquid.

2 To make sauce, place undrained tuna, anchovies, lemon juice and capers in a blender or food processor and process, gradually adding oil, until mixture is creamy. Transfer mixture to a bowl, add mayonnaise and stir until combined. Season to taste with pepper. Reserve and refrigerate 1/2 cup (125 mL) sauce for garnish.

3 Remove chicken from liquid and cut into thick slices or chunks. Arrange a layer of chicken on serving dish and spread with sauce to thickly coat. Top with remaining chicken and sauce, repeating layers. Cover chicken and let marinate for 2 hours at room temperature or refrigerate overnight.

4 Stir reserved sauce and spread over chicken. Garnish with lemon wedges, capers, olives and parsley and bring to room temperature. Serve with salad greens and sautéed vegetables.

Serves 8

Grilled Quail with Wild Rice Pilau

6	quail	6
1 tsp	rosemary	5 mL
1 tbsp	olive oil	15 mL
	freshly ground black pepper	
PILAU		
1 cup	wild rice	250 mL
1 cup	long-grain rice	250 mL
3 cups	water	750 mL
1 tbsp	butter	15 mL
1 tsp	salt	5 mL
1/4 cup	olive oil	60 mL
1 oz	pine nuts	30 g
2 tbsp	currants	30 mL

◆ ◆ ◆

1 Split each quail down backbone, spread out and flatten breast with broad side of a meat cleaver. Season with rosemary and pepper to taste. Brush with 1 tbsp (15 mL) olive oil. Place on a plate and allow to marinate for 30 minutes at room temperature.

2 Place all rice, water, butter and salt in a heavy-based saucepan. Bring to a boil, stir and cover. Reduce heat and simmer gently for 20 minutes. Remove lid. Fluff rice with a fork.

3 Heat oil in a skillet, add pine nuts and currants and cook, stirring, for 5 minutes or until golden. Toss mixture with rice.

4 Cook quail under a preheated broiler for 3-4 minutes on each side or until cooked as desired. To serve, pile rice on a heated plate and arrange quail on top.

Serves 6

Fresh Fruit with Mascarpone

1	mango, peeled	1
2	peaches	2
2	nectarines	2
1/2 lb	cherries, pitted	225 g
1/2 lb	fresh raspberries or blueberries	225 g
3 tbsp	orange juice	45 mL
2 tbsp	liqueur of your choice (optional)	30 mL
1 cup	mascarpone or sour cream	250 mL
1 tbsp	brown sugar	15 mL

◆ ◆ ◆

1 Slice and pit mango, peaches and nectarines, and place in a bowl with cherries and berries. Sprinkle over orange juice and liqueur, if desired. Cover with plastic wrap and refrigerate, stirring occasionally, for several hours to allow flavors to mellow.

2 Place mascarpone or sour cream in a bowl, add sugar and mix to combine.

3 Serve fruit on flat dessert plates with mascarpone and accompany with almond-flavored cookies, if desired.

Serves 6

Poached Salmon *with* Mango Mint Sauce

3 cups	water or half white wine, half water	750 mL
1 tbsp	vinegar (omit if wine is used)	15 mL
1	onion, sliced	1
5-6	parsley sprigs	5-6
1	thyme sprig	1
1	bay leaf	1
6	peppercorns	6
1 tsp	salt	5 mL
3 lbs	fresh center-cut salmon or ocean trout	1.5 kg
1	cucumber, thinly sliced	1
	mango slices and salad greens	

MANGO MINT SAUCE

1	mango	1
1 1/2 cups	light olive oil	375 mL
1/2 cup	balsamic or red wine vinegar	125 mL
8	fresh mint leaves, shredded	8

1 Preheat oven to 325°F (160°C). Bring water, and wine or vinegar, onion, parsley, thyme, bay leaf, peppercorns and salt to a boil, then simmer for 10 minutes. Pour into a non-metallic baking dish large enough to hold fish.

2 Place fish on a rack in dish, cover with foil and bake, basting every 15 minutes, for 30-35 minutes or until tender.

3 To make sauce, cut flesh from mango, place in a food processor and process, gradually adding oil, then vinegar and mint leaves, until smooth and thick.

4 Carefully lift fish from liquid and remove skin. Place fish on a serving dish, decorate with cucumber slices and serve with mango slices, salad greens and sauce.

Serves 8

♦ ♦ ♦

Avocado Julienne Salad

1	red or green bell pepper	1
1	carrot	1
4	green onions	4
2	avocados, halved and pitted	2

MUSTARD DRESSING

2 tbsp	olive oil	30 mL
1 tbsp	wine vinegar	15 mL
1 tbsp	balsamic vinegar	15 mL
2 tsp	rum (optional)	10 mL
1 tsp	Dijon mustard	5 mL
	freshly ground black pepper	
	dash Tabasco sauce	

1 Cut red pepper, carrot and green onions into thin julienne strips. Blanch strips in boiling water for a few seconds, then drain, rinse and pat dry with paper towels. Place in a bowl.

2 To make dressing, place oil, vinegars, rum (if desired) and mustard in a screwtop jar with pepper and Tabasco sauce to taste. Shake well to combine. Pour over vegetables and toss.

3 To serve, pile vegetables into avocado halves.

Serves 4

♦ ♦ ♦

Warm Fish Salad *with Green Aioli*

3 tbsp	butter	45 mL
1	garlic clove, bruised	1
1 lb	firm white fish fillet, cut into	450 g
	3/4 inch (2 cm) squares	
	watercress	

GREEN AIOLI

3	egg yolks	3
3 tbsp	chopped parsley	45 mL
3 tbsp	chopped basil	45 mL
2 tbsp	chopped chives	30 mL
2 tbsp	lemon juice	30 mL
1	garlic clove, crushed	1
1 cup	oil	250 mL

1 Arrange watercress on a serving plate. Melt butter in a large skillet over low heat. Add garlic and cook for 1 minute without burning. Remove garlic with a slotted spoon.

2 Raise heat to medium, add fish pieces and stir-fry until cooked through. Using slotted spoon, transfer fish to serving plate.

3 To make aioli, combine egg yolks, fresh herbs, lemon juice and crushed garlic in a blender or food processor. Process briefly to blend. With motor running, gradually add oil, drop by drop, then in a steady stream, until mixture thickens to consistency of mayonnaise.

4 Spoon a little of the aioli over fish. Serve at once, offering remaining aioli separately.

Serves 4

◆ ◆ ◆

Tomato, Corn *and Shrimp Salad*

2 1/2 cups	cooked or drained canned corn kernels	625 mL
1	onion, finely chopped	1
1/2 lb	peeled cooked shrimp, cut into	225 g
	1/2 inch (1 cm) lengths	
2	tomatoes, chopped	2
3	green onions, chopped	3
1	red bell pepper, finely chopped	1
2 tbsp	red wine vinegar	30 mL
2 tbsp	olive oil	30 mL
1	garlic clove, crushed	1
1 tbsp	lemon juice	15 mL
	chopped fresh parsley	

1 Combine corn, onion, shrimp, tomatoes, green onions and red pepper in a salad bowl. Mix well.

2 Mix vinegar, oil, garlic and lemon juice in a screwtop jar. Close lid tightly, shake dressing well and pour over salad. Toss to coat. Serve topped with chopped parsley.

Serves 4

◆ ◆ ◆

Seafood Terrine

1 lb	white fish fillets, skinned	450 g
2	egg whites, lightly whipped	2
1 1/2 cups	whipping cream	375 mL
2 tbsp	lemon juice	30 mL
1/2 lb	peeled cooked shrimp, chopped	225 g
3	large zucchini, thinly sliced	3
	lemon and fresh herbs for garnish	

♦ ♦ ♦

1 Preheat oven to 325°F (160°C). Cut fish into small pieces, removing any bones, and purée in a blender or food processor. Press purée through a sieve into a bowl.

2 Set bowl over ice, add egg whites and cream and beat mixture with a wooden spoon until thick. Beat in lemon juice.

3 Brush a loaf pan with oil, line with wax paper and brush with oil again.

4 Spoon half the fish purée into a separate bowl and stir in shrimp. Spread half the plain fish purée over base of loaf pan, arrange half the zucchini slices on top, then spread half the shrimp mixture over zucchini.

5 Add a second layer of zucchini slices followed by remaining shrimp mixture. Spread rest of the plain fish purée on top, cover terrine with foil and place in a roasting pan. Add boiling water to come halfway up sides of terrine.

6 Bake for 30 minutes. Leave terrine to cool for 10 minutes before removing from pan. Serve chilled or at room temperature. Garnish with lemon wedges and fresh herbs, if desired.

Serves 6-8

Cold Garlic Shrimp with Avocado

2	ripe avocados, halved, peeled and pitted	2
1 lb	peeled cooked shrimp, deveined, tails intact	450 g
1	large onion, cut into thin rings	1
3	garlic cloves, crushed	3
2 tbsp	olive oil	30 mL
1/4 cup	lemon juice	60 mL
2 tbsp	white wine vinegar	30 mL
1 tbsp	chopped fresh parsley	15 mL

♦ ♦ ♦

1 Slice avocados neatly and arrange on a serving plate with shrimp and onion rings.

2 Whisk garlic, olive oil, lemon juice and vinegar together in a small bowl. Pour over salad and sprinkle with parsley. Serve.

Serves 4

Rice and Pepper Terrine

1 tbsp	butter	15 mL
1	onion, chopped	1
2 1/2 cups	cooked rice	625 mL
1 cup	milk	250 mL
3	eggs	3
1 tsp	hot pepper sauce, or to taste	5 mL
1/3 cup	grated Pecorino or Parmesan cheese	85 mL
2 tbsp	chopped fresh parsley	30 mL
3	roasted red bell peppers, peeled and sliced	3

◆ ◆ ◆

1. Preheat over to 350°F (180°C). Melt butter in a medium skillet, add onion and cook until tender.

2. In a large bowl, combine rice, milk, eggs, pepper sauce, cheese, parsley and cooked onion. Mix well.

3. Grease and line a loaf pan. Spoon one third of rice mixture into pan. Top with half the roasted pepper slices, then a further third of rice mixture. Top with remaining peppers and rice.

4. Bake for 35-40 minutes. Cool for 10 minutes before removing from pan. Serve warm or cold.

Serves 8

TIP: To roast peppers, place them whole under a preheated broiler, and broil, turning from time to time, until skin is charred on all surfaces. Place peppers in a paper bag until cool, then rub off charred skin and cut out seeds and membranes.

Eggplant Ratatouille

2 lbs	baby eggplant, halved, or 1 large eggplant, cut into strips	1 kg
2	onions, sliced	2
4	garlic cloves, peeled	4
2 lbs	young green beans, trimmed	1 kg
4	ripe tomatoes, quartered	4
1/2 cup	olive oil	125 mL
1/2 cup	pitted black olives	125 mL
4-5 tbsp	chopped fresh parsley	60-75 mL
	salt and freshly ground black pepper	

◆ ◆ ◆

1 Sprinkle eggplant liberally with salt and spread out on a large glass dish. Top with another dish to weigh it down lightly, tip at an angle (put a wooden spoon under one end) and let stand for 30 minutes. Rinse under running water, drain and dry on paper towels.

2 Place onion in a large, heavy-based saucepan and sprinkle with salt and pepper. Top with garlic, then beans, eggplant and tomatoes, seasoning each layer. Pour oil evenly over vegetables.

3 Cover pan and bring to a boil, then turn down heat and simmer gently for 40 minutes or until vegetables are tender. Garnish with olives and parsley. Serve with new potatoes.

Serves 8

Mediterranean-Style Stuffed Peppers

8	red or green bell peppers	8
1 1/2 tsp	salt	7 mL
2 tbsp	olive oil	30 mL
1/2 cup	boiling water	125 mL

RICE STUFFING

1 cup	rice	250 mL
1/4 cup	olive oil	60 mL
2	onions, finely chopped	2
2 tbsp	pine nuts	30 mL
1 tsp	salt	5 mL
1 cup	undrained canned tomatoes	250 mL
1/2 cup	boiling water	125 mL
1 1/2 oz	currants or chopped raisins	45 g
1/4 tsp	ground allspice	1 mL
1/4 tsp	freshly ground black pepper	1 mL
2 tsp	sugar	10 mL
2 tbsp	chopped fresh mint	30 mL

♦ ♦ ♦

1 To make stuffing, place rice in a bowl, pour on enough boiling water to cover, and let stand until water cools. Drain, rinse with cold water and drain again.

2 Heat oil in a saucepan, add onions, pine nuts and salt and cook, stirring, until onions are golden. Add rice and stir until well coated with oil. Add tomatoes, boiling water, currants or raisins, allspice, pepper, sugar and mint. Reduce heat, cover and cook for 15 minutes or until liquid is absorbed. Cool completely.

3 Cut tops off peppers and remove seeds. Loosely fill with stuffing. Arrange, close together, in a heavy-based saucepan and sprinkle with salt and olive oil. Pour in 1/2 cup (125 mL) boiling water, cover and simmer for 25-30 minutes or until tender. Add more water, if necessary, to avoid burning. Cool in saucepan, then refrigerate until served.

Serves 8

Peperonata

2 tbsp	olive oil	30 mL
3 tbsp	butter	45 mL
2	large onions, chopped	2
6	red and/or green bell peppers, cut into strips	6
2	garlic cloves, crushed	2
6	ripe tomatoes, peeled and quartered	6
2 tbsp	fresh basil or oregano leaves	30 mL
	salt and freshly ground black pepper	

♦ ♦ ♦

1 Heat oil and butter in a heavy-based skillet over medium heat. Add onions and cook, stirring, until soft and golden. Add peppers and garlic to pan, season to taste with salt and pepper, cover and simmer for 15 minutes.

2 Add tomatoes to pan, stir well and cook over low heat, uncovered, for 30 minutes or until peppers are tender and mixture is thickened. Add basil or oregano just before serving.

Serves 6

TIP: Peperonata stores well in the refrigerator, covered, and is nice to have on hand as a side dish or for part of an antipasto platter. Try slices in cold meat sandwiches.

MEDITERRANEAN-STYLE STUFFED PEPPERS

Mixed Vegetable Salad

1 lb	frozen broad beans or lima beans, cooked	450 g
2	small carrots, diced and cooked	2
3	thinly sliced celery stalks	3
1	red bell pepper, chopped	1
1	green bell pepper, chopped	1
6-8	green onions, finely chopped	6-8
2 cups	canned corn kernels, drained	500 mL
1 1/2 cups	canned red kidney beans, rinsed and drained	375 mL
	Vinaigrette Dressing (see below)	
1/2 cup	chopped fresh parsley	125 mL
3 tbsp	chopped fresh mint or basil	45 mL

1 Place broad beans, carrots, celery, red and green pepper, green onions, corn and kidney beans in a large bowl.

2 Prepare vinaigrette, pour over salad and mix well. Set aside to marinate at least 30 minutes at room temperature, or several hours in refrigerator. Sprinkle with herbs and toss before serving.

Serves 10

♦ ♦ ♦

Tortellini Salad

1 lb	frozen tortellini or other filled pasta	450 g
6	sun-dried tomatoes, sliced	6
3	stalks celery, sliced	3
8-10	black olives	8-10
3 tbsp	chopped fresh parsley	45 mL
1 tbsp	chopped fresh basil	15 mL

VINAIGRETTE DRESSING

2 tsp	Dijon mustard	10 mL
1 tbsp	tarragon vinegar	15 mL
1/3 cup	olive oil	85 mL
1 tsp	salt	5 mL
	freshly ground black pepper	

1 Cook tortellini in boiling, salted water following package directions until *al dente*. Drain well.

2 To make dressing, place mustard, vinegar, oil, salt and pepper to taste in a large bowl and whisk until well combined. Add hot pasta, toss to coat and set aside to cool.

3 Add sun-dried tomatoes, celery and olives to pasta, mix well and transfer to serving bowl. Top with parsley and basil. Toss lightly before serving.

Serves 6

♦ ♦ ♦

Crunchy Potato Salad

5	large potatoes, peeled and cubed	5
1/2 cup	pickled onions, drained	125 mL
8	hard-boiled eggs, in wedges	8
2 tbsp	drained capers	30 mL
1/2 cup	roasted peanuts	125 mL
1/2 cup	olive oil	125 mL
	salt and freshly ground black pepper	

♦ ♦ ♦

1 Cook potatoes in a pot of lightly salted boiling water until tender. Drain and let cool to room temperature. Place in a salad bowl with onions, eggs, capers and peanuts. Drizzle olive oil over salad, season to taste and toss.

Serves 4

Pepper and Mushroom Salad

4	red and green bell peppers	4
1/2 lb	fresh mushrooms, sliced	225 g
2	garlic cloves, crushed	2
2 tbsp	red wine vinegar	30 mL
1 tbsp	olive oil	15 mL
1 tsp	crushed black peppercorns	5 mL

♦ ♦ ♦

1 Steam peppers over boiling water for 5 minutes. Cool slightly and cut into thin strips. Mix with mushrooms in a bowl.

2 Whisk remaining ingredients together in a small bowl. Pour dressing over salad and toss well.

Serves 4

BARBECUE
COOKING

There are few meals more enjoyable than a relaxing barbecue — and few culinary experiences more catastrophic than the cookout that turns into a flaming disaster. So how do you plan the perfect al fresco meal?

Whether your barbecue is a handy hibachi, a convenient gas barbecue or a thing of brick-built beauty, the site for your fire is all important. It should be in as sheltered a position as possible, but away from obvious hazards like overhanging branches or adjacent bushes.

Always take care when cooking on the barbecue. Ensure that children and animals are kept well away from the area. Use long, preferably wooden-handled tools. Never leave a fire unattended and smother the fire after cooking.

GINGER CHICKEN (TOP), STEAKS ON THE BARBECUE, FOIL BARBECUED POTATOES (PAGE 39)

BARBECUE KNOW-HOW

PLANNING
The best barbecue cooks take their time getting organized: stocking up on charcoal, hickory chips and firelighters; making special marinades and sauces; making sure all necessary tools, including metal spatula and tongs, are at hand, and remembering not only the matches for starting the fire, but also a water pistol for dousing unwanted flames.

COOKING
As with other forms of cooking, practice makes perfect. Impatience is a common fault. Most fires should be lit at least 45 minutes before cooking is to commence; briquettes are ready when they are ash-grey all over, with glowing hearts. Only then should the coals be spread out for cooking; close together (but not a solid mass) for intense, concentrated heat; spread out for more gentle heat over a wider area. When using a rotisserie, or when cooking roasts, it is usual to cook by indirect heat; either arranging the coals in a ring or placing them towards the back of the barbecue. A pan may be placed under the roast to catch the juices.

Most barbecues have grills whose height above the fire can be adjusted. Other ways of controlling the degree of heat include changing the shape of the fire, adding or subtracting fuel and using a windbreak.

THE FOOD
A wide range of foods can be successfully cooked on the barbecue, including fish, meats (steaks, chops, sausages, burgers, kebabs —even whole roasts), vegetables and fruit.

FISH
Fish is one of the great successes of the barbecue story, but the secret is in the selection (choose firm fish for cooking directly over the coals; wrap the more delicate varieties in foil) and in sensitive heat control. Fish should be cooked over medium, not fierce heat, so either allow the initial heat of the coals to subside somewhat, or raise the grill. Crisp, lightly charred skin improves the flavor of oily fish like sardines; move them nearer to the heat source for the final few minutes of cooking.

Even over relatively low heat, fish cooks swiftly. If cooking a whole fish, slash the skin in several places, through to the bone, to conduct the heat efficiently. Check frequently and remove the fish from the heat source as soon as the flesh flakes readily when tested with the tip of a knife. The flesh of even the more robust varieties is delicate, so take particular care when turning fish; hinged grills are an inexpensive and highly successful solution to the problem, but, as with any surface with which the fish comes into contact, they must be well oiled before use. If cooking whole fish, place the tail ends towards the hinge.

COOKING WITH HERBS
The wonderful aroma of fresh herbs is entirely in keeping with the outdoor aspect of barbecue cookery. Add finely chopped parsley, tarragon, chervil or chives to foil parcels; make fresh herb stuffings, thread bay leaves on kebab skewers or simply toss fresh dill, rosemary, thyme or fennel directly onto the coals towards the end of cooking.

POULTRY
Poultry is delicious when cooked on the barbecue. Chicken wings, with plum sauce or marinated in raspberry vinegar and oil, make an inexpensive and tasty meal for all the family. Chicken quarters and drumsticks are also ideal barbecue candidates, but take care that breasts do not overcook.

MEAT
Flares are most definitely to be avoided. The aim is to cook by controlled heat, charring the meat but avoiding the burnt offerings that result from sudden bursts of flame caused by fat dripping on the coals. Always trim excess fat from meats, especially lamb and pork, and use good quality low-fat ground beef for burgers.

VEGETABLES AND FRUIT
Zucchini can be cooked whole on the barbecue, or share a skewer with tomatoes, peppers, eggplant cubes and mushrooms for a vegetarian treat. For a simple taste sensation, cook matchsticks of root vegetables (carrots, parsnips, turnips) in foil parcels with a spoonful of butter and a sprinkling of fresh herbs.

As for fruit, banana and pineapple have a special affinity for fireside meals.

MICROWAVE MAGIC
The microwave is a wonderful aid to better barbecuing. Items such as chicken drumsticks or thighs can be partially cooked in the microwave before being finished off on the barbecue grill, thus ensuring that the poultry is perfectly cooked all the way through — and saving both time and energy.

Sausages can be given the same treatment, but items such as chicken breasts and steaks, which cook quickly over hot coals, should not be precooked.

Steaks on the Barbecue

1/3-1/2 lb	steak per person	150-225 g
	vegetable or olive oil	
	marinade or seasoning (optional, see below)	

♦ ◆ ♦

1 For individual steaks, cut meat 1 inch (2.5 cm) thick. If cooking meat in a single large piece, cut it 1 1/2-2 inches (4-5 cm) thick. Marinate or season (if desired) before cooking. Place meat on an oiled rack 3 inches (7 cm) above moderately hot coals. Sear steaks quickly on both sides to seal in juices, then move to a cooler area of rack and barbecue until cooked as desired, turning once. Serve immediately.

MARINADES AND SEASONINGS

The following quantities are enough for 4 steaks or 2 lbs (1 kg) meat.

• **Wine Marinade:** Combine 1 cup (250 mL) red or white wine, 1 sliced onion, 1 tsp (5 mL) black peppercorns, 1 bay leaf, 4 parsley sprigs, 1/2 tsp (2 mL) dried thyme and 1/4 cup (60 mL) oil. Marinate steak or chicken for 1 hour at room temperature or for several hours in refrigerator.

• **Mustard Steak:** Beat 1/4 lb (110 g) butter with 1 tbsp (15 mL) dry mustard and spread over steak.

• **Pepper Steak:** Press coarsely ground black pepper into steak on both sides and let stand for 30 minutes.

• **Herbed Steak:** Rub steaks with olive oil, then crumbled rosemary, thyme or oregano.

Ginger Chicken

1/4 cup	soy sauce	60 mL
2 tbsp	grated fresh ginger	30 mL
1 tbsp	honey	15 mL
1/4 tsp	freshly ground black pepper	1 mL
3 lbs	chicken pieces	1.5 kg

♦ ◆ ♦

1 Combine soy sauce, ginger, honey and pepper in a shallow dish, add chicken and marinate for 1-2 hours, turning once or twice. Drain, reserving marinade.

2 Grill chicken over hot coals, turning and basting with marinade, for 20 minutes or until tender and well glazed.

Serves 4

Foil Barbecued Potatoes

1 Scrub medium-size baking potatoes and cook in boiling water for 20 minutes. Drain, dry well, rub with a little butter or oil and wrap each potato in foil. Cook potatoes in coals or on barbecue grill, turning occasionally, for 20 minutes or until tender when pierced with a skewer. To serve, pull back foil, cut a cross in top of each potato, squeeze open and season or fill as desired.

Butterflied Leg of Lamb

1	leg of lamb, butterflied	1
1/4 cup	fresh lemon juice	60 mL
2 tsp	ground coriander	10 mL
1 tsp	ground cardamom	5 mL
1 tsp	ground cumin	5 mL
1/2 tsp	ground turmeric	2 mL
1/2 cup	plain yogurt	125 mL
	salt and freshly ground black pepper	

♦ ♦ ♦

1 Lay meat flat and slash any thick portions not quite through. Place in a large shallow dish. Rub lemon juice, spices, salt and pepper to taste on all surfaces, then brush with yogurt and set aside to marinate for 1-2 hours, turning once or twice.

2 Lift meat from marinade and place, skin-side-down, on an oiled grill rack about 4 inches (10 cm) above medium coals. Cook, turning and basting occasionally with remaining marinade, for 1 hour or until cooked to taste. To carve, start at one end and slice across grain.

Serves 6

NOTE: A leg of lamb (boned, with seam left open), barbecued flat on the grill, will cook in less than an hour to a rich brown outside with thin portions well done and thick portions slightly pink.

Marinated Grilled Chicken

2	2 lb (1 kg) chickens, split in 2	2

SOY GINGER MARINADE

1/4 cup	dry vermouth	60 mL
1/4 cup	soy sauce	60 mL
1 tbsp	brown sugar	15 mL
2 tbsp	grated fresh ginger	30 mL
1/4 tsp	freshly ground black pepper	1 mL

♦ ♦ ♦

1 To make marinade, place vermouth, soy sauce, sugar, ginger and pepper in a deep bowl and stir to combine. Place chickens in marinade, turn to coat well and set aside to marinate, turning once or twice, for 1-2 hours at room temperature.

2 Drain well, reserving marinade. Cook chickens over hot coals, turning and basting with marinade, for 20 minutes or until cooked and well glazed. Test by inserting a skewer into thickest part of flesh; juices should run clear.

Serves 4

Pepper Beef Fillet *with* Watercress Sauce

4 tbsp	butter, softened	60 mL
2	garlic cloves, crushed	2
3 tbsp	crushed black peppercorns	45 mL
1 1/2 lbs	beef fillet, trimmed	675 g
4 oz	watercress	110 g
1	egg yolk	1
2 tsp	Dijon mustard	10 mL
1/4 tsp	salt	1 mL
1/4 tsp	grated nutmeg	1 mL
3/4 cup	light olive oil	185 mL
1 tbsp	freshly squeezed lime juice	15 mL
1/4 cup	whipping cream	60 mL

◆ ◆ ◆

1 Preheat oven to 350°F (180°C). Beat butter and garlic together in a small bowl. Spread out crushed peppercorns on a piece of foil. Coat meat with garlic butter and roll in peppercorns.

2 Cook beef fillet on a rotisserie, or on an oiled rack over hot coals, turning frequently, until done to taste. Transfer to a plate, cover with a tent of foil and let stand for 10 minutes.

3 Set aside about a third of the watercress for garnish. Strip remaining leaves from stems for sauce.

4 Combine egg yolk, mustard, salt and nutmeg in a blender or food processor. Process until smooth. With motor running, add oil through the feeder tube, at first drop by drop, then in a steady stream. When sauce starts to thicken, add watercress leaves and process until finely chopped. Transfer sauce to a bowl, beat in lime juice, then add cream and mix well.

5 Slice beef. Fan out slices on a plate garnished with reserved watercress. Spoon a little of the watercress sauce down center of meat slices. Serve remaining sauce separately.

Serves 4

Barbecued Beef Stuffed with Herbed Vegetables

1 tbsp	butter	15 mL
1	onion, chopped	1
2	garlic cloves, crushed	2
1	red bell pepper, chopped	1
1	large zucchini, finely diced	1
1	large carrot, finely diced	1
3 tbsp	chopped fresh herbs	45 mL
2/3 cup	fresh white breadcrumbs	165 mL
1/3 cup	grated Parmesan cheese	85 mL
2 lb	piece of rump steak, about 2 inch (5 cm) thick	1 kg
1/4 cup	olive oil	60 mL
2 tbsp	Dijon mustard	30 mL
2 tbsp	crushed black peppercorns	30 mL
1/4 cup	red wine	60 mL

1 To make stuffing, heat butter in a skillet over medium heat. Add onion, garlic and pepper and cook for 1 minute. Stir in zucchini and carrot and cook for 3 minutes more. Finally stir in herbs. Turn off heat, stir in breadcrumbs and cheese then allow mixture to cool to room temperature.

2 Insert a knife into side of steak, cutting almost, but not quite through to other side, to form a pocket. Stuff vegetable mixture firmly into pocket and close opening with string.

3 Mix oil, mustard, pepper and wine in a bowl. Grill steak over moderately hot coals until cooked as desired, basting frequently with oil mixture and turning every 15 minutes.

Serves 6

◆ ◆ ◆

Moroccan Brochettes

3 lbs	boned lamb, cut from leg or shoulder	1.5 kg
2	onions, quartered	2
2	green bell peppers, cut into squares	2

GINGER AND CUMIN MARINADE

1/4 cup	lemon juice	60 mL
2 tbsp	olive or vegetable oil	30 mL
1	small onion, grated	1
1 tsp	salt	5 mL
1 tsp	ground cumin	5 mL
1 tsp	grated fresh ginger	5 mL
	freshly ground black pepper	

♦ ♦ ♦

1 To make marinade, place lemon juice, oil, grated onion, salt, cumin, ginger and pepper to taste in a ceramic or glass bowl and stir to combine. Trim excess fat from lamb and cut into large cubes. Add lamb to marinade, stir to coat well and set aside to marinate for at least 2 hours.

2 Separate onion quarters into petals. Thread meat onto skewers alternating with pepper squares and onion pieces, not too closely together.

3 Cook kebabs on an oiled rack over hot coals, turning frequently, for 8-10 minutes or until lamb is crusty brown on outside but still pink in center.

Serves 8

Tabbouleh

3/4 cup	bulghur	185 mL
10	green onions, finely chopped	10
1 1/2 cups	chopped flat-leaf parsley	375 mL
6 tbsp	chopped fresh mint	90 mL
2	firm, ripe tomatoes, chopped	2
3 tbsp	vegetable oil	45 mL
1/4-1/2 cup	lemon juice	60-125 mL
	salt and freshly ground black pepper	
	lettuce leaves (optional)	

♦ ♦ ♦

1 Soak bulghur in cold water for 1 hour. Drain well and squeeze out excess liquid. Place in a bowl, cover and refrigerate for 1 hour.

2 Add green onions to bulghur and mix well, crushing with back of a spoon to slightly bruise onions. Add parsley, mint, tomatoes, oil and lemon juice and mix thoroughly. Season to taste with salt and black pepper.

3 Line a salad dish with lettuce leaves, if desired, and spoon in Tabbouleh.

Serves 6

NOTE: *Bulghur is a quick-cooking form of wheat made from precooked, dried and cracked wheat grains. You can usually find it in natural food stores or gourmet sections of supermarkets.*

Pork and Stuffed Pepper Kebabs

2 lbs	pork fillet, cut into 1 1/2 inch (4 cm) cubes	1 kg
12	small bay leaves	12
2	red bell peppers, each cut into 6 wide strips	2
1 1/4 cups	dried breadcrumbs	310 mL
1	small onion, finely chopped	1
2 tbsp	chopped fresh mint or coriander	30 mL
1/2 tsp	ground cumin	2 mL
1 tbsp	lemon juice	15 mL
3-4 tbsp	butter, melted	45-60 mL

MINT AND GARLIC MARINADE

1/2 cup	olive oil	125 mL
1/4 cup	fresh lemon juice	60 mL
1/4 cup	white or red wine	60 mL
2 tbsp	chopped fresh mint or coriander	30 mL
3	garlic cloves, crushed	3
	salt and freshly ground pepper	

♦ ♦ ♦

1 Combine all marinade ingredients in a bowl and stir well. Add pork cubes, cover and set aside to marinate for 2 hours. Drain well, reserving marinade.

2 Blanch red pepper strips in a saucepan of simmering water for 3-5 minutes. Drain and pat dry on paper towels. Place breadcrumbs, onion, mint, cumin and salt and pepper to taste in a bowl, add lemon juice and mix with enough melted butter to make a mixture that holds together. Roll tablespoons of the mixture into pepper strips and thread 2 rolls alternately with 2 bay leaves and 3 cubes of pork onto each of 6 skewers.

3 Cook on an oiled grill rack over medium coals, turning occasionally and basting with marinade, for 20-25 minutes, or until pork is cooked through and golden. Serve with pita bread and tomato salad.

Serves 6

Spicy Chicken Satay with Peanut Sauce

6	chicken breast fillets, cut into cubes	6
2	onions, chopped	2
2	garlic cloves, crushed	2
1 tbsp	very finely chopped lemon grass	15 mL
1 tsp	ground coriander	5 mL
1 tsp	ground cumin	5 mL
2 tsp	grated fresh ginger	10 mL
1/4 cup	vegetable oil	60 mL

PEANUT SAUCE

1	onion, chopped	1
6	hot red chili peppers, chopped	6
3/4 cup	peanuts	185 mL
1/4 cup	oil	60 mL
1 tbsp	tamarind sauce	15 mL
2/3 cup	water	165 mL

1 Arrange chicken in a single layer in a shallow bowl. Combine onions, garlic, lemon grass, spices and oil in a blender or food processor and process until smooth. Pour over chicken, stir to coat, then cover and refrigerate for 4-8 hours. Drain chicken cubes, discarding marinade. Thread cubes onto oiled metal or soaked wooden skewers and set aside.

2 To make sauce, combine onion, chili peppers and peanuts in a blender or food processor and process until smooth. Heat oil in a saucepan, add onion mixture and cook, stirring, for 5 minutes. Add tamarind sauce and water and bring to a boil. Lower heat and simmer until sauce has reduced and thickened.

3 Cook chicken on an oiled rack over hot coals until tender and golden brown. Serve with peanut sauce.

Serves 8

♦ ♦ ♦

Italian Grilled Chicken on Greens

1/4 cup	fresh lemon juice	60 mL
1/2	onion, finely chopped	1/2
1-2 tbsp	olive oil	15-30 mL
1-2	garlic cloves, crushed (optional)	1-2
1 tsp	dried oregano	5 mL
2	small chickens, quartered	2
	assorted salad greens	
	salt and freshly ground black pepper	

♦ ♦ ♦

1 Combine lemon juice, onion, oil, garlic (if desired), oregano, salt and pepper to taste in a large shallow glass dish. Add chicken, turning to coat, and set aside to marinate for at least 1 hour.

2 Drain chicken, reserving marinade. Place, skin-side-down, on an oiled grill rack over moderately hot coals and cook for 5 minutes. Turn, baste with marinade, and cook for 10 minutes more. Turn again and cook 5 minutes, or until chicken is tender and juices run clear. Serve on a bed of mixed greens.

Serves 4

TIP: Be bold in your choice of greens, selecting for color, flavor and texture. For the photo, we used butter lettuce, watercress and radicchio.

Melon and Berries

1	small cantaloupe, quartered	1
2 cups	strawberries, halved	500 mL
1 cup	blueberries	250 mL
2 tbsp	icing sugar	30 mL
2 tbsp	white rum or orange-flavored liqueur	30 mL

♦ ♦ ♦

1 Slice flesh off melon wedges, cube flesh and replace in melon shells. Place berries in a bowl, add icing sugar and rum or liqueur and gently toss to coat. Spoon berries over melon wedges and serve.

Serves 4

Broiled Basil Chicken Drumsticks

8	chicken drumsticks	8
2 tbsp	butter, softened	30 mL
2 tbsp	chopped fresh basil	30 mL
2 tbsp	chopped pine nuts	30 mL
1/3 cup	Cheddar cheese, grated	85 mL
1 tbsp	finely chopped fresh parsley	15 mL

♦ ♦ ♦

1 Bring a large saucepan of water to a boil. Add chicken and allow water to return to boiling point. Lower heat and simmer for 10 minutes. Drain chicken and cool slightly.

2 Mix remaining ingredients in a small bowl and spread between skin and flesh on each drumstick.

3 Grill on an oiled grill rack over hot coals, brushing frequently with any remaining butter mixture, until golden and cooked through.

Serves 4

Grilled Citrus Chicken

2	large oranges	2
1	small red onion, sliced into thin rings	1
1 tbsp	sherry	15 mL
4-6	chicken pieces	4-6
1 tbsp	vegetable oil	15 mL
1 tbsp	lemon juice	15 mL
	salt	
	parsley or watercress for garnish	

◆ ◆ ◆

1 Using a vegetable peeler, thinly peel rind from oranges and cut rind into julienne strips. Place strips and onion in a bowl, add sherry and set aside to marinate.

2 Brush chicken with oil, sprinkle with half the lemon juice and season with salt to taste. Grill, skin-side-down, over moderately hot coals on an oiled rack, turning and brushing frequently with oil, for 15-20 minutes or until tender.

3 Remove all pith from oranges and cut into thin slices. Place chicken on a heated plate. Sprinkle orange strips, onion rings and remaining lemon juice on top, surround with orange slices, and garnish with parsley or watercress.

Serves 4

Charcoal Grilled Shrimp

30-36	raw medium shrimp	30-36
1 tbsp	finely chopped fresh ginger	15 mL
2 tbsp	finely chopped fresh parsley	30 mL
1	bay leaf	1
1/2 tsp	chopped fresh thyme or 1/4 tsp (1 mL) dried thyme	2 mL
1/4 tsp	dried, crushed red chili peppers	1 mL
2 tbsp	olive oil	30 mL
2 tbsp	fresh lemon juice	30 mL
6 tbsp	butter	90 mL
1	garlic clove, crushed	1
	salt and freshly ground black pepper	

♦ ◆ ♦

1 Using kitchen shears, cut along back rim of each shrimp and rub gently under cold running water to remove black vein. Pat dry on paper towels. Peel shrimp, if desired, but leave tail segments intact.

2 Place shrimp in a large bowl, sprinkle with ginger, parsley, bay leaf, thyme, dried chili peppers, and salt and pepper to taste. Add oil and lemon juice, mix well and set aside to marinate at room temperature for 30 minutes.

3 Drain shrimp and place on an oiled grill rack over moderately hot coals. Cook for 2 minutes. Turn and cook 2-3 minutes longer or until shrimp curl and turn pink. Meanwhile, melt butter with garlic in a small saucepan. When bubbling, discard garlic, pour over shrimp and serve immediately.

Serves 6

Grilled Tomatoes

6	firm, ripe tomatoes	6
1/4 cup	olive oil	60 mL
2 tbsp	finely chopped fresh basil	30 mL
	salt and freshly ground black pepper	

♦ ◆ ♦

1 Neatly core tomatoes and cut in half crosswise. Arrange halves, cut-side-up, on an oiled grill rack or hotplate over medium coals. Brush with oil and sprinkle with salt and pepper to taste. Cook, turning once or twice, for 3-5 minutes or until heated through. Sprinkle with basil and serve immediately.

Serves 6

TIP: Slice 6 small zucchini lengthwise, rub them with olive oil and herbs, and add them to the barbecue with the tomatoes. Turn them once or twice until tender-crisp.

Salmon with Lime Butter Baste

6 tbsp	butter	90 mL
1	garlic clove, crushed	1
1/4 cup	freshly squeezed lime juice	60 mL
2 tsp	grated lime rind	10 mL
2 tsp	grated lemon rind	10 mL
1 tbsp	dry white wine	15 mL
2 tsp	honey	10 mL
1 tbsp	chopped fresh parsley	15 mL
4	salmon fillets, 8 oz (225 g) each	4

1 Melt butter in a small saucepan over medium heat. Stir in garlic and cook for 1 minute. Add lime juice, lime rind, lemon rind, wine and honey and mix well. Stir in parsley.

2 Cook salmon fillets on an oiled grill rack over moderately hot coals, brushing frequently with lime butter baste, for about 3 minutes on each side or until cooked through.

Serves 4

TIP: You can cook any firm fish using this method. Swordfish is particularly good when barbecued.

Mixed Seafood Skewers

12	sea scallops, rinsed and deveined	12
12	large raw shrimp, peeled and deveined, tails intact	12
2	firm fish fillets, cut into 3/4 inch (2 cm) cubes	2
4 tbsp	butter	60 mL
3 tbsp	fresh lemon juice	45 mL
1	garlic clove, crushed	1
1/4 tsp	freshly ground black pepper	1 mL
2 tbsp	each chopped fresh chervil, dill and thyme	30 mL

◆ ◆ ◆

1 Keeping types of seafood separate, thread scallops, shrimp and fish cubes onto 12 small oiled metal or soaked wooden skewers.

2 Melt butter in a small saucepan. Stir in lemon juice, garlic and pepper. Brush each kebab generously with mixture. Sprinkle chervil over scallops, dill over shrimp and thyme over fish cubes.

3 Grill kebabs over moderately hot coals for about 2 minutes each side or until tender.

Serves 4

TIP: Use a firm fish such as salmon or swordfish for the fish kebabs. If you are lucky enough to find scallops with the lovely coral-colored roe still attached, thread it onto the skewers along with the scallops, as shown. Delicious!

Salad
Main Attractions

Sometimes, when the weather seems to stay hot forever, it is almost impossible to work up any enthusiasm for turning on a stovetop burner, much less the oven. And our enthusiasm for eating a hot or rich meal is equally restricted.

Those are the days when a main course salad is the only sensible solution — and this chapter contains enough ideas to carry you through a serious heatwave!

When it comes to salads, bear in mind that the most important rule is to use the freshest possible ingredients. So always feel free to change the ingredients depending on what you find at the produce counter.

SHRIMP SALAD (TOP), SPRING SALAD (PAGE 58)

Shrimp Salad

1	head lettuce	1
1	onion, sliced in rings	1
1/2 lb	cherry tomatoes	225 g
2	carrots, quartered lengthwise, then sliced	2
2	red bell peppers, cut into thin strips	2
40	peeled cooked large shrimp, deveined, tails intact	40
1/4 cup	lemon juice	60 mL
1/2 tsp	chili sauce	2 mL
1/4 cup	olive oil	60 mL
	freshly ground black pepper	

1 Tear lettuce into pieces and spread on a large plate. Arrange vegetables and shrimp on top.

2 Mix lemon juice and chili sauce in a bowl. Whisk in oil. Add pepper to taste. Pour over salad just before serving.

Serves 4

♦ ◆ ♦

Spring Salad

1	head curly endive, torn into pieces	1
1	radicchio lettuce, separated into leaves	1
12	tender young asparagus spears, trimmed and cut into 2 inch (5 cm) lengths	12
12	canned artichoke hearts, halved	12
4	carrots, cut into thin strips	4
3	hard-boiled eggs, sliced	3
1/2 cup	olive oil	125 mL
1/4 cup	white wine vinegar	60 mL
2 tbsp	drained capers	30 mL

1 Arrange endive and radicchio leaves on a large plate.

2 Blanch asparagus in boiling water for 1 minute then refresh under cold water and drain thoroughly.

3 Arrange asparagus, artichoke halves, carrots and hard-boiled eggs on lettuce.

4 Whisk oil and vinegar in a bowl, stir in capers and add to salad. Toss well.

Serves 4

♦ ◆ ♦

Vegetable Beef Salad

2 tbsp	butter	30 mL
3/4 lb	beef fillet	350 g
1 cup	peeled winter squash, cut into strips	250 mL
1 cup	green beans, topped and tailed	250 mL
4	small custard squash, quartered or zucchini, sliced	4
2 tbsp	diced red bell pepper	30 mL
3 tbsp	olive oil	45 mL
1	garlic clove, crushed	1
1 tbsp	red wine vinegar	15 mL
	freshly ground black pepper	

♦ ◆ ♦

1 Preheat oven to 350°F (180°C). Melt butter in a skillet over high heat. Add beef fillet and sear until browned on all sides, about 5 minutes.

2 Transfer fillet to a baking dish and roast for 30 minutes or until cooked as desired.

3 Meanwhile, bring a large saucepan of water to a boil. Add winter squash, beans and custard squash or zucchini. Cook for 2 minutes. Drain, refresh under cold running water and drain again.

4 Cut beef into thin slices and place in a salad bowl. Add vegetables and red pepper.

5 Mix olive oil, garlic, vinegar and pepper in a screwtop jar. Close lid tightly and shake dressing until well mixed. Pour over salad and toss well. Serve from bowl or on individual plates.

Serves 4

Potato and Smoked Sausage Salad

1 lb	new potatoes, scrubbed and halved	450 g
3 tbsp	oil	45 mL
1 tsp	salt	5 mL
1 lb	smoked pork sausages	450 g
6	chopped green onions	6
2 tbsp	chopped chives	30 mL
1	garlic clove, crushed	1
2 tsp	fresh lemon juice	10 mL
6 tbsp	plain low-fat yogurt	90 mL
6 tbsp	sour cream	90 mL

◆ ◆ ◆

1 Preheat oven to 400°F (200°C). Bring a large saucepan of water to a boil. Add potatoes and parboil for 10 minutes. Drain. Toss potatoes in 2 tbsp (30 mL) oil, sprinkle with salt and spread out in a roasting pan. Roast for 30 minutes or until golden brown and crisp, turning occasionally.

2 Meanwhile, heat smoked sausages, following instructions on package. Heat remaining oil in a skillet or wok. Add onions and stir-fry for 1 minute. Transfer to a serving bowl. Add roast potatoes.

3 Remove skin from each sausage, slice thinly and add to bowl. Toss mixture lightly and arrange on a serving plate. Blend or process chives with garlic, lemon juice, yogurt and sour cream until smooth. Pour over salad, garnish with whole chives and serve.

Serves 4

TIP: *Fresh asparagus, cut into lengths and stir-fried with the green onions makes a delicious variation of this salad.*

Fettucine, Ham and Pepper Salad

1/2 lb	fettucine	225 g
2	yellow and/or red bell peppers, halved	2
2	thick slices smoked ham, slivered	2
1/4 lb	Gruyère cheese, cubed	110 g
6-8	black olives, pitted and quartered	6-8

Mustard Vinaigrette

1 1/2 tsp	Dijon mustard	7 mL
1 tbsp	wine vinegar	15 mL
1/2	garlic clove, crushed	1/2
3 tbsp	olive oil	45 mL
	freshly ground black pepper	

♦ ♦ ♦

1 Cook fettucine in boiling salted water following package directions until *al dente*. Drain well and set aside.

2 Place peppers under a preheated broiler and cook until skins blacken and blister. Seal peppers in a paper bag and set aside until cool enough to handle. Peel off and discard skins and cut flesh into long strips.

3 To make vinaigrette, place mustard in a bowl, add vinegar, garlic and pepper to taste and whisk to combine. Gradually add oil, whisking until dressing thickens.

4 Place peppers, ham, Gruyère cheese and olives in a salad bowl. Add vinaigrette and pasta and mix lightly to combine. Cover and chill for at least 1 hour before serving.

Serves 6

Basque Rice Salad

¹/₂ tsp	saffron filaments or pinch of saffron powder	2 mL
¹/₄ cup	olive oil	60 mL
1	bunch green onions, thinly sliced	1
2 cups	white rice	500 mL
4 cups	chicken stock	1 L
1 tsp	salt	5 mL
¹/₄ lb	salami, cut into strips	110 g
1 lb	cooked shrimp, shelled and deveined	450 g
2	red and/or green bell peppers, cut into thin strips	2
4 tbsp	chopped fresh parsley	60 mL
	freshly ground black pepper	
	lemon wedges	

♦ ♦ ♦

1 If using saffron filaments, soak in just enough warm water to cover for 5 minutes.

2 Heat oil in a large saucepan over medium heat and cook green onions until soft. Add rice and stir until grains are well coated with oil. Add stock, salt and saffron. Stir once, cover tightly and bring to a boil. Reduce heat and simmer on low for 20 minutes or until rice is tender and liquid is absorbed.

3 Remove lid and let rice stand a few minutes. Fluff up rice with a fork and turn into a bowl.

4 Add salami, shrimp, peppers and parsley to rice, season with salt and pepper to taste and toss well to combine. Arrange on a large plate. Serve at room temperature with lemon wedges to squeeze over salad.

Serves 8

Pasta *and* Salami Salad

¹/₂ lb	large shell macaroni	225 g
3 tbsp	olive oil	45 mL
2	garlic cloves, crushed	2
1 oz	pine nuts	30 g
¹/₄ lb	salami, sliced	110 g
1 tbsp	chopped fresh parsley	15 mL

❖ ◆ ❖

1 Cook macaroni in boiling salted water following package directions until *al dente*. Drain.

2 Heat oil in a large skillet over medium heat. Add garlic and pine nuts and cook, stirring constantly, for 1 minute or until pine nuts are golden. Remove pan from heat, stir in salami, parsley and pasta and serve warm or at room temerature.

Serves 4

Chicken Potato Salad with Thyme and Mayonnaise

1 lb	cooked chicken, cut into bite-size pieces	450 g
4	zucchini, grated	4
1 tsp	chopped fresh thyme	5 mL
8	new potatoes, boiled, halved	8
1	red bell pepper, sliced into thin strips	1
1 tbsp	chopped fresh coriander	15 mL
4	hard-boiled eggs, sliced	4
4 tbsp	**Vinaigrette** (see p. 66)	60 mL
2 tbsp	**Mayonnaise** (see p. 66)	30 mL

◆ ◆ ◆

1 Combine chicken, zucchini, chopped thyme and potatoes in a bowl and mix well.

2 Arrange chicken mixture on serving plates. Top with red pepper strips, coriander and egg slices.

3 Mix vinaigrette and mayonnaise in a small bowl, then pour over salad. Serve chilled, garnished with a sprig of thyme.

Serves 4

Pasta Salad with Smoked Sturgeon

¹/₂ lb	fusilli pasta	225 g
¹/₂ lb	smoked sturgeon or smoked trout	225 g
8	sun-dried tomatoes in oil, halved	8
12-16	small black olives	12-16
1	small red onion, sliced	1
	salad greens, prepared and crisped	
	lemon, cut into wedges	

Mustard Chutney Dressing

2 tsp	Dijon mustard	10 mL
¹/₃ cup	virgin olive oil	85 mL
2 tsp	balsamic vinegar	10 mL
1 tbsp	mayonnaise (see p. 66)	15 mL
1 tbsp	fruit chutney	15 mL

1 Cook pasta in boiling salted water until *al dente*. Drain and refresh under cold water, drain again and place in a bowl.

2 To make dressing, place mustard in a small bowl and gradually add oil, whisking until mixture thickens. Whisk in vinegar, then mayonnaise and chutney. Toss through pasta and set aside to marinate for 30 minutes.

3 Remove skin and any bones from fish, and slice. Add to pasta mixture with tomatoes, olives and onion and toss lightly.

4 Line dinner plates with salad greens, top with pasta mixture and garnish with lemon wedges.

Serves 4

♦ ◆ ♦

Mayonnaise

2	egg yolks	2
1/4 tsp	sugar	1 mL
1/2 tsp	salt	2 mL
1/2 tsp	dry mustard	2 mL
1 tbsp	lemon juice	15 mL
1 tbsp	white wine vinegar	15 mL
1 cup	vegetable and/or olive oil	250 mL

1 Combine egg yolks, sugar, salt, mustard and 1 tsp (5 mL) each of the lemon juice and vinegar in a bowl.

2 Whisk mixture until it thickens, then add oil, drop by drop, whisking constantly and making sure that each drop of oil is incorporated before adding the next. When about half the oil has been added and mayonnaise is thick, remaining oil may be added in a steady stream.

3 Alternatively, make mayonnaise in a blender or food processor. The process is virtually the same: start by blending egg yolk mixture, then, with motor running, add oil through feeder tube, at first drop by drop, then in a steady stream. Finally, beat or blend in remaining lemon juice and vinegar.

Makes about 1 1/4 cups (310 mL)

KITCHEN TIP: If the mayonnaise shows signs of curdling, try whisking in 1 tsp (5 mL) of boiling water before adding more oil. If that fails, beat a fresh egg yolk in a clean bowl. Whisk in about 1 tsp (5 mL) of the curdled mixture. Still whisking, add the rest of the mayonnaise drop by drop, checking that each drop of curdled mixture is incorporated before adding more.

Vinaigrette

2 tbsp	wine vinegar	30 mL
1 tsp	Dijon mustard	5 mL
1/4 tsp	salt	1 mL
6 tbsp	olive oil	90 mL
	freshly ground black pepper	

1 Combine vinegar and mustard in a small bowl. Add salt and pepper to taste. Gradually whisk in oil. Alternatively, mix all ingredients in a screwtop jar, and shake until well mixed.

Makes about 3/4 cup (185 mL)

Monkfish and Spinach Salad with Mango

2 tsp	light olive oil	10 mL
3 tbsp	soy sauce	45 mL
1 tbsp	honey	15 mL
1/4 tsp	crushed black peppercorns	1 mL
1/4 cup	red wine vinegar	60 mL
4	monkfish fillets, about 5 oz (150 g) each, cut into 3/4 inch (2 cm cubes)	4
1	red bell pepper, seeded and cut into strips	1
1	bunch fresh spinach leaves, torn into bite-sized pieces	1
1	mango, pitted and peeled, cut into cubes	1

◆ ◆ ◆

1 Heat oil in a large skillet over medium heat. Add soy sauce, honey, pepper and red wine vinegar and cook for 1 minute.

2 Add fish pieces and cook for 3-5 minutes, or until cooked. Remove fish and set aside.

3 Add red pepper to skillet and cook for 3 minutes, stirring occasionally.

4 Arrange spinach leaves, mango, red pepper and fish pieces in a serving bowl, and toss gently.

Serves 4

FRESH FRUIT
FINALES

Perfectly fresh, ripe raspberries, strawberries, blueberries, peaches and pears are among the fleeting pleasures of summer. What better way to take advantage of summer's abundance than by showcasing these treasures in stunningly simple desserts?

And the recipes in this chapter carry the added bonus of being easy on the cook! Just one tip — before you plan your menu, find out what fruits are at their peak in your own area, and select a recipe to match. Imported fruits have their place in our kitchens, but there is nothing to match the flavor of food locally grown and freshly picked!

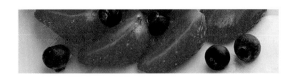

PINEAPPLE ICE, PEACH COOLER WITH WHIPPED CREAM (PAGE 78)

Mixed Berry Meringues with Apricot Coulis

3	egg whites, at room temperature	3
5 tbsp	sugar	75 mL
1 tsp	vanilla extract	5 mL
1 cup	raspberries	250 mL
1 cup	blueberries or pitted black cherries	250 mL
3 tbsp	Grand Marnier	45 mL
1 cup	canned apricot halves, drained	250 mL
1/4 cup	apricot and orange nectar	60 mL
6	fresh mint sprigs to decorate	6

♦ ♦ ♦

1 Preheat oven to 300°F (150°C). Using an electric mixer, beat egg whites until light and fluffy. Gradually add sugar, beating constantly.

2 Add vanilla and beat for 10 minutes more until mixture is thick and glossy.

3 Place mixture in a piping bag. Pipe six nests, about 2 1/2 inches (6 cm) in diameter, on a baking sheet lined with wax paper.

4 Bake for 20 minutes, then lower oven temperature to 250°F (120°C) and bake for 25 minutes more. Cool on baking sheet.

5 In a small bowl, combine raspberries, blueberries or cherries and Grand Marnier.

6 To make the coulis, purée apricot halves with apricot and orange nectar in a blender or food processor.

7 To assemble dessert, spoon 2 tbsp (30 mL) of apricot coulis onto each serving plate. Fill each meringue nest with berry mixture, place one nest on each plate and decorate with fresh mint. Serve at once.

Serves 6

TIP: If you want egg whites to beat up properly, be sure to beat them in a completely clean, grease-free bowl. Plastic bowls tend to absorb grease permanently, so do not use them for beating egg whites.

MIXED BERRY MERINGUES WITH APRICOT COULIS

Fig and Walnut Mousse

6	fresh or canned figs	6
1 1/2 cups	whipping cream	375 mL
1 tbsp	vanilla extract	15 mL
2 tbsp	icing sugar, sifted	30 mL
4 oz	walnuts, roughly chopped	120 g
	fig slices and chopped walnuts for garnish	

♦ ◆ ♦

1 Spoon out fig flesh and break up with a fork.

2 Whip cream together with vanilla extract and sugar until thick. Fold in fig pulp and walnuts, spoon into serving glasses and decorate each with a slice of fig and a piece of walnut.

Serves 4-6

Fruit with *Vanilla Cream*

2	mangoes	2
2	kiwis	2
2 cups	strawberries	500 mL
1 cup	whipping cream	250 mL
1/2 cup	sour cream	125 mL
2 tbsp	icing sugar, sifted	30 mL
1 tsp	vanilla extract	5 mL

♦ ♦ ♦

1 Arrange fruit on four serving plates. Whip cream until thick, fold in sour cream and add icing sugar and vanilla extract. Chill until ready to serve.

Serves 4

TIP: This simple dessert depends on presentation, and looks most dramatic when served on plates that provide a contrast to the jewel tones of the fruit.

Glazed Fresh Strawberry Tart

PASTRY

1 ¹/₂ cups	all-purpose flour	375 mL
¹/₂ tsp	salt	2 mL
6 tbsp	butter or margarine	90 mL
	ice water	

FILLING

4 cups	small strawberries, hulled	1 L
³/₄ cup	sugar	185 mL
2 tbsp	cornstarch	30 mL
2 tbsp	strained strawberry jam or any red fruit jelly	30 mL
1 cup	water	250 mL
2 tsp	fresh lemon juice	10 mL
2 tbsp	strawberry-flavored jelly powder	30 mL

◆ ◆ ◆

1 Preheat oven to 375°F (190°C). Combine flour and salt in a large bowl. Cut in butter with a knife until mixture resembles coarse breadcrumbs. Stir in enough ice water to make a firm dough.

2 Roll out dough on a lightly floured surface to fit a 9 inch (23 cm) quiche pan or pie plate. Line pastry with wax paper, then fill with dried beans. Bake for 15 minutes or until golden. Cool.

3 In a medium saucepan, bring sugar, cornstarch, jam or jelly, water and lemon juice to a boil, stirring constantly. Cook for 2 minutes, then stir in jelly powder until dissolved. Cool.

4 Spoon half of jelly mixture into pastry shell, arrange strawberries on top, then glaze with remaining jelly mixture. Cool, then chill until set.

Serves 8

TIP: Use any dried beans as baking weights, but don't try to cook them after they have been baked!

Apricot Bavarian

8	apricots, pitted and chopped	8
1/2 oz	powdered gelatin	15 g
1/4 cup	apricot nectar or orange juice	60 mL
1 cup	whipping cream	250 mL
1 oz	pistachio nuts	30 g
	sliced apricots	

◆ ◆ ◆

1 Blend or process apricots until quite smooth. Sprinkle gelatin onto apricot nectar or orange juice in a bowl. When spongy, set bowl over a saucepan of simmering water until gelatin has dissolved. Stir gelatin into apricot purée. Let cool. Whip cream until thick, then fold into apricot mixture.

2 Pour into 4 lightly oiled, 1/2-cup (125 mL) molds and refrigerate until set. Serve with fresh apricot slices, whipped cream and pistachio nuts.

Serves 4

Pear and *Peach Champagne Sherbet*

14 oz	can pears, drained and chopped	398 mL
14 oz	can peaches, drained and chopped	398 mL
1/2 cup	sugar	125 mL
2/3 cup	champagne	165 mL

◆ ◆ ◆

1 Process fruit in a blender or food processor until smooth.

2 Combine sugar and champagne in a large saucepan. Simmer over low heat until sugar has dissolved.

3 Stir in puréed fruit. When cool, pour mixture into a freezer-proof container. Cover and freeze for 3 hours or until partially set.

4 Remove sherbet from freezer and break up ice crystals with a fork. Return sorbet to freezer until firm. Serve in scoops, decorated with strips of lime zest if desired.

Serves 6

Summer Fruit Cheesecake

1 cup	crushed plain vanilla wafers	250 mL
2 tbsp	brown sugar	30 mL
4 tbsp	butter, melted	60 mL

CHEESE FILLING

10 oz	cream cheese or Neufchâtel cheese	300 g
1/2 cup	sugar	125 mL
2	eggs, separated	2
1 1/2 tsp	grated orange rind	7 mL
1 tbsp	powdered gelatin	15 mL
3-4 tbsp	freshly squeezed orange juice	45-60 mL
2 tbsp	freshly squeezed lemon juice	30 mL
1 1/4 cups	whipping cream, whipped	310 mL

SUMMER FRUIT TOPPING

2-3 cups	prepared mixed fresh fruit	500-750 g
1/3 cup	water	85 mL
1/3 cup	strained fresh orange juice or 2 tbsp (30 mL) lemon juice	85 mL
2 tbsp	sugar	30 mL
2 tsp	arrowroot blended with 1 tbsp (15 mL) cold water	10 mL

◆ ◆ ◆

1 To make base, place cookie crumbs, brown sugar and butter in a bowl and mix until well combined. Press mixture into base of an oiled 8 inch (20 cm) springform pan and chill until firm.

2 To make filling, beat cheese in a mixing bowl until light and fluffy. Gradually add sugar, then egg yolks and orange rind, beating until fluffy. Soak gelatin in orange juice in a small bowl over simmering water and stir until dissolved. Stir gelatin mixture and lemon juice into cheese mixture, then fold in whipped cream.

3 Beat egg whites to stiff peaks and lightly fold into cheese mixture. Pour mixture into prepared pan and chill until firm, several hours or overnight.

4 To make topping, wash and prepare fruit and set aside. Heat water, orange or lemon juice and sugar in a saucepan over medium heat, stirring until sugar dissolves and mixture forms a light syrup. Stir in arrowroot mixture and cook, stirring constantly, until thickened and bubbly. Remove from heat, stir in fruit and cool.

5 Remove cheesecake from pan and place on serving plate. Top with fruit and serve.

Serves 8

TIP: For this recipe, try whole blueberries, raspberries or strawberries, peeled sliced peaches, plums, mangoes, or sliced kiwis or grapes.

Peach Cooler *with* Whipped Cream

4	ripe peaches, peeled, pitted and sliced	4
1 cup	sweet white wine such as riesling, moselle or sauterne	250 mL
2 tbsp	brandy	30 mL
1 tbsp	fresh lime or lemon juice	15 mL
	sugar	
	grated fresh nutmeg for garnish	

WHIPPED CREAM TOPPING

1 1/4 cups	whipping cream	310 mL
2 tbsp	icing sugar	30 mL
1 tbsp	fresh lime or lemon juice	15 mL

◆ ◆ ◆

1 Place peaches in a non-metallic bowl; add wine, brandy, lime or lemon juice and sugar to taste and stir lightly to dissolve sugar. Cover and refrigerate for at least 1 hour.

2 To make topping, beat cream with icing sugar until mixture begins to stiffen. Add lime or lemon juice and continue beating until stiff.

3 To serve, spoon peaches with liquid into serving glasses and top with dollops of cream. Garnish with nutmeg and serve decorated with a mint leaf or tiny flower, if desired.

Serves 4

Pineapple Ice

2 tsp	powdered gelatin	10 mL
1/4 cup	water	60 mL
1 cups	sugar	250 mL
4 cups	water	1 L
1 cup	drained canned crushed pineapple	250 mL
1/3 cup	lemon juice	85 mL

◆ ◆ ◆

1 Set freezer at coldest setting. Soften gelatin in 1/4 cup (60 mL) water. Place sugar and 4 cups (1 L) water in a saucepan over medium heat and stir until sugar dissolves. Bring to a boil then boil, without stirring, for 5 minutes. Remove pan from heat, add gelatin mixture and stir until dissolved.

2 Transfer mixture to a bowl and chill for 45-60 minutes or until mixture begins to thicken. Stir in pineapple and lemon juice. Pour mixture into 1 deep or 2 shallow freezer trays and freeze until mushy.

3 Place mixture in a chilled bowl and beat with electric or rotary beater until smooth. Return to pans and freeze, stirring several times, until firm.

4 To serve, break up mixture with a fork and scoop into wine glasses or serving bowls. Garnish with mint or pineapple leaves, if desired.

Serves 6

NOTE: *You must use canned pineapple for this recipe. Fresh pineapple will not produce a satisfactory result.*

Banana and Raspberry Sherbets

3	ripe bananas	3
6 tbsp	fresh lemon juice	90 mL
1 cup	whipping cream	250 mL
1	pinch cinnamon	1
3 cups	fresh raspberries	750 mL
SYRUP		
2 cups	sugar	500 mL
2 cups	water	500 mL

◆ ◆ ◆

1 To make syrup, combine sugar and water in a heavy-based saucepan. Stir over low heat until sugar dissolves, then bring mixture to a boil and cook for 5 minutes without stirring. Remove syrup from heat and let cool to room temperature.

2 To make banana sherbet, purée bananas in a food processor or blender with 2 tbsp (30 mL) of lemon juice until creamy. Add cream, cinnamon and 1 cup (250 mL) of the syrup, then process for 30 seconds. Transfer banana sherbet mixture to an ice cream churn and process according to manufacturer's instructions.

3 To make raspberry sherbet, purée raspberries in a food processor or blender. Strain purée to remove raspberry seeds. Stir remaining lemon juice into strained purée. Add 1 cup (250 mL) of the syrup and stir well. Discard any remaining syrup or reserve for use in another recipe. Transfer raspberry sherbet mixture to an ice cream maker and freeze according to manufacturer's instructions. Serve scoops of sherbet with fresh fruit and a sprig of mint.

Serves 6

INDEX